CLINTON

PORTRAIT OF VICTORY

CLINTON
PORTRAIT OF VICTORY

Photographs by

P. F. Bentley

on assignment for TIME magazine

Prologue by Roger Rosenblatt

Epilogue by Michael Kramer

Text by Rebecca Buffum Taylor

Photo Selection by Alex Castro

An Epicenter Communications Book

WARNER BOOKS

A Time Warner Company

With special thanks to all those at TIME magazine and in the Clinton-Gore campaign whose enthusiasm and support helped make this project possible.

Created and Produced by
EPICENTER COMMUNICATIONS
Sausalito, California 94965

EPICENTER COMMUNICATIONS:

    President: Matthew Naythons, MD
    VP, Executive Editor: Rebecca Buffum Taylor
    Art Director: Alex Castro
    Project Manager: Dawn Sheggeby
    Editorial Assistant: Kate Warne
    Administrative Assistant: Erika Gulick Smith

WARNER BOOKS, INC.
    Time & Life Building
    1271 Avenue of the Americas
    New York, NY 10020

WARNER BOOKS
A Time Warner Company

Printed in the United States of America
First Printing: January 1993

10 9 8 7 6 5 4 3 2 1

ISBN: 0-446-51758-5
LC: 92-62438

Prologue
In Black and White

Roger Rosenblatt

A presidential campaign comes to the people in color on television and in magazines, which makes it all the more odd how colorless campaigns can seem. There is something numbing and emotionally draining about the proliferation of reds, whites, and blues—more so, perhaps, because these are the colors of American patriotism. When they are blared day in and day out, not only do people lose their enthusiasm for a campaign, but they feel a kind of embittered weariness, as if the colors, always on the edge of becoming clichés in themselves, helped to make a cliché of the entire process of choosing a president, a cliché even of the country.

This is not so when things are shown in black and white. The use of black-and-white is rare these days; by its contrast from the norm, it draws one's attention automatically. It is also a remnant of the past—the only way life used to be represented on film or television, or in photographs. In some way, black-and-white both speaks a reverence for the past and re-creates it, brings the mind back to a slower, more studied pace. It makes one want to look into, not merely at, a picture, and to stay awhile.

See P. F. Bentley's photograph of Bill Clinton giving a speech with the American flag concealing all of his body except for the pants cuffs, shoes, and a gesturing arm. The picture demands one's concentration because it is not in color, though the scene, of course, was. The black-and-white recapitulates the event to emphasize its meaning. "What is going on?" one is impelled to ask. A campaign speech, to be sure, but something more. If one did not know who the particular candidate in this photograph was, it might be said that he is wrapping himself in the flag. Yet Bill Clinton was attacked during the campaign for being *un*-American; as a student he avoided the draft, he visited Moscow.

The irony of the image is compounded by the fact that Clinton supported and helped pass an ordinance against flag-burning in the state of Arkansas. What sort of candidate, then, is gesturing to the crowd? A flag-burner? A flag-waver? Something more complicated? What sort of a relationship to the flag do people want of their candidate? Or, to take the picture literally: What sort of flag is gesturing to the crowd?—since what one sees is a flag making a speech.

Then look at the crowd, their clothes and faces. Could they not be a political audience of the 1940s or 1950s, of almost any era really? One begins to dream back into the entire history of presidential campaigns, the history of American politics itself—all because the black-and-white depiction has removed the distraction of color. Yet somehow black-and-white makes the color more vivid, because one knows that the color is there without seeing it there. Recall the movie *The Manchurian Candidate*, particularly the furious spectacle of the final scenes of the nominating convention. Many people to this day are surprised to be reminded that the movie was shot in black-and-white.

The striking power of black-and-white, as this book illustrates, is that it probes the inner life of things, always mysterious. Black-and-white produces ambiguity, produces gray. An unconscious thought process provokes the mystery: "What I am seeing in black-and-white is not really black and white, therefore it must be something else. What is it?" Color in general is bad for mystery (see the "colorizations" of *The Asphalt Jungle* or *The Maltese Falcon*). It is especially bad for human mystery, because it announces by its very colorfulness that all one sees is out in the open.

Black-and-white announces the opposite. One craves the inner life of a presidential campaign because the participants are engaged in an effort to conceal the inner life, to put a "spin" on all images, and because the outer life is usually so stupid. The campaign of 1992 was often very stupid, with its concentration on Gennifer and Jennifer and Dan Quayle's hot potatoe [*sic*], at the expense of discussions of the economy, education, the poor, and the people. One will notice a great many shadows in these photos. When the substance of an event has been so insubstantial, it is a relief and a pleasure to view the shadows.

So what does one see in these pictures? What *was* the Clinton campaign of 1992, as viewed through Bentley's and his Leica's eye?

From one angle it appears an exhibit of the machinery of connection—telephones in limousines, on floors, on walls, hand-held phones, bouquets of microphones, microphones on stands, on poles. Someone, including Bill Clinton, is always on the horn to somewhere else, his voice carried somewhere else. The candidate must be in several places at once, must be alert to, and informed of, several things at once. He must live in a multitude of tenses and situations. Bentley has caught something about these broadcasting devices: they connect to everything but the here and now. By so doing they serve as emblems of the dangers of the presidency itself. So focused on reelection are today's politicians, their campaigns have become substitutes for governing. For a president as well as a candidate it is a struggle to live in the here and now.

The machinery of transportation—another element of these pictures—also takes the candidate away from present time and place. Modern campaigns are reported in terms of movement and travel: "On the Road with the Candidate"; "On the Plane with the President." High-speed travel is necessary when one has to cover a vast country over a short period of time, but in modern campaigns it has become something of an end in itself.

One of the very good ideas of the Clinton campaign, it seems to me, was the bus tour—not only because it brought the candidate into closer contact with people in small places, but because it was slow. People seem increasingly interested in slowing down these days. Forced by economic straits to pull back and in, they are reminded of the virtue by necessity. These still photos are such reminders.

The shadows themselves become items in this theme of motion against motion, time against time. In the Hiroshima Peace Memorial Museum, an institution built to commemorate the consequences of the first A-bomb, are photographs of the shadows that victims left on walls and on bridges when the people themselves had been obliterated. Bentley's shadows stretch out from the candidate and his entourage, as if clinging to the ground that will only be occupied by the group for a moment, then vacated as the caravan moves on. Not only are these, too, symbols of wanting to hold things in place for a while, but they are shadows of the future. This campaign is likely to be the first and last time citizens will feel so close to the Clinton presidency. Isolated by the nature of his job, he will never seem as near to people again. The shadows cling to the ground; the people cling to the shadows.

The effect of these various elements is strangely contradictory. The pictures clearly show the verve, hustle, energy, occasionally the joy, of the enterprise of running for president: Hillary Clinton's animated face in the middle of a thousand on-the-run conversations; her husband about to clap his hands enthusiastically, or listening with bemused intent as a potential voter gesticulates; aides clowning; kids playing; all that.

At the same time, there is an undercurrent of melancholy, enforced by the machines and the shadows, and read in the faces of the principals even as they smile. On some level, Bentley's photographs are not images of a campaign, but rather of people involved in, and trapped by, a campaign. They did not invent the process in which they are participating. They are traditionalists operating within a convention, and they must make the convention their own. Think what it must be like, embarking on the endless series of talks, embraces, conferences, interviews, *photographs*—the repetition of questions and observations; the repetition of jokes and "spontaneous" wisecracks; the image of oneself, reproduced ad nauseam on placards, on TV.

How many hundreds of times has Clinton looked out on crowds such as these and seen a gigantic field whose sole crop was his name on sticks? I think of children writing their own names over and over in notebooks, staring at the letters with a mixture of pride and confusion, possession and distance. At some extravagant, celebratory moment, when the candidate looked out on all the representations of his name bobbing up and down in front of him, did he ever wonder, "Who is this Clinton?"

Though they are devoted to the soul of the campaign, and not to its political narrative, Bentley's pictures do convey some of the campaign's more significant moments. The early photos taken in New Hampshire show all the fatigue that both Clintons had to feel as they headed into the winter of the venture. In those days not only was Bill Clinton behind in the polls, but he wasn't even his party's candidate. In those days, there were the Flowers tapes and the first accusations about the draft. Those were defensive, and testing, days. One reads the dark strain of that time both in what one sees in these pictures and in what one imagines happening outside the pictures—when Clinton sat alone, out of reach even of Bentley, and despaired and fought despair.

It is interesting to speculate if a similar set of photographs, taken a few years from now during the Clinton administration, would look anything like the ones in this book. Surely, Bill Clinton will look different. Once he is actually in charge of the country, rather than working toward being in charge of the country, both he and Hillary will be so elevated in the world's eye, it will be terribly difficult to see into their lives.

Perhaps the most important and turnaround moment in the early days of the campaign occurred between Clinton and Jesse Jackson. Whatever else the American people search for in their presidential candidates, one indispensable quality is nerve. It took nerve for Clinton to speak out against Sister Souljah's inflammatory rap lyrics in the wake of the Los Angeles riots, more nerve still to do his speaking at a convention before a black audience, and in the presence of Jesse Jackson, who, until this campaign, was regarded as—and saw to it that he was regarded as—the portal to every black voter in the country.

Clinton's courage involved not only facing down Jackson per se, which would have been pointless and merely macho, but it was a statement as well—the first such made by a Democratic candidate in many years—that black Americans were not to be treated as some bloc-vote property, but were to be accorded the dignity of being seen as individuals. Yes, it was thinkable that a Democratic candidate could criticize a black celebrity in public for trying to stir up trouble, just as he might criticize a white. And it was thinkable that he could do so under the eye of Jesse Jackson.

So look at the picture of the two of them, not quite silhouetted before the window over the city. If ever there were a classic demonstration of body language, it is Jackson's: the somber face, the folded arms, the stiff back and neck. You can feel his muscles contract.

And then there are the pictures of Hillary Clinton. One that is particularly striking is also particularly ordinary: a huddle of the Clintons with their senior strategists, standing in a circle and making plans. Clinton is listening to his wife, who clearly has the floor. "Buy one, get one free," they used to say good-naturedly but not jokingly, at the outset of the campaign, though they stopped saying such things once the Republicans started going after Hillary. She had a weird view of family, they said. In her legal and policy writings, they said, she encouraged children to sue their parents. She was an "activist," or worse, "a feminist."

Either the accusations were untrue or so simplified as to be meaningless. But accusations aside, everyone could see that Hillary Clinton was bound to make a formidable First Lady. Not Barbara Bush, Nancy Reagan, Rosalynn Carter, or even Eleanor Roosevelt had the kind of substantive influence on the White House that Hillary Clinton undoubtedly would have. Here was someone who had actually made public policy herself, not simply cajoled her husband into making it. Here, too, was both a professional woman and a working wife and mother, come to prominence at a time when women long to see how the competitive strands of a woman's life may be woven together. No wonder her husband listens to her.

The picture of the campaign huddle, the picture of Clinton and Jesse Jackson, of the machinery of the campaign, the crowds, the flag—all are presented here as if one merely stumbled across these various scenes, so invisible is the photographer. After the Clintons gave Bentley permission to hang around the campaign and shoot at will, they appeared to forget about him. Bentley told Matthew Naythons—another life-probing photojournalist, whose company produced this book project—that he and Clinton would speak to each other about once a week. Yet Bentley was around a great deal more than that.

He was there and he wasn't there—a magic act that gives these photos an innocent look. Oddly, even the ones in which people pose deliberately have that same quality—as if the subjects had rigged a shutter, then had run around in front of the camera. The black-and-white itself—to return to that subject—aids Bentley's own unobtrusiveness. If color is the new journalism of photography, in which the photographer's presence is always loudly proclaimed, black-and-white is the old journalism, in which the photographer disappears, and things speak for themselves.

One of six Democratic hopefuls at the start of the race, Clinton formally declared his candidacy in October 1991, when George Bush's approval ratings were at a formidable 75%. Embarking on one of the most grueling presidential campaigns ever run, the candidate fields questions from the press in Detroit. 13 March 1992

Unfettered, unorthodox, and at times unnerving, James Carville, Clinton's chief strategist, immediately takes the offensive after the *Wall Street Journal* broke its draft-letter story, raising questions about the 1969 letter Clinton wrote to an ROTC officer and implying that Clinton had dodged the Vietnam draft. "We are going to release this letter to every paper in New Hampshire," Carville told Clinton, defending his candidate's patriotism. Communications Director George Stephanopoulos looks on. 12 February 1992

Facing the second trust crisis in his campaign—the Gennifer Flowers story had surfaced in January—Clinton prepares to face new attacks on his electability. Here Carville and Stephanopoulos discuss the draft-dodging allegations in a senior citizens' center laundry room while Clinton addresses its members next door. Later, Carville questions Clinton on what he remembers of the events surrounding the ROTC letter in the hallway of their Manchester hotel, as Stephanopoulos and Campaign Director Bruce Lindsey plan their responses to this new setback. 11 and 14 February 1992

A Yale Law graduate twice ranked one of the country's one hundred top attorneys and a tireless advocate for education reform and children's rights, Hillary Clinton campaigned alongside her husband from the start; here the pair listens to locals over coffee at Kay's Restaurant in Hudson, New Hampshire. 17 February 1992

In what would become the Year of the Woman in American politics, Hillary talks with a Manchester voter while canvassing house-to-house for the primary. 15 February 1992

Following page: Amid the fears and flurries of their winter campaign, the Clintons create a moment of intimacy on a late-night flight home. 13 February 1992

Struggling to emerge from the shadows that dogged him through his first primary, Clinton phones Ted Koppel from Springfield, Vermont, about his appearance that evening on *Nightline* to discuss the draft-letter issue. The governor's ratings had plummeted 20% in a free-fall after the 1969 letter surfaced, but leveled out again a few days after his Koppel interview. 12 February 1992

The morning of the New Hampshire primary, Clinton rallies voters in Concord while Trip Director Bruce Garamella confirms the next two days' schedule with Little Rock headquarters. "We worked hard," Clinton said of his multi-town, tarmac-to-tarmac, first primary, "and what we proved was that the American people were hungry for an honest discussion of the issues." 18 February 1992

Finally able to relax after the New Hampshire results are in, Clinton calls his daughter, Chelsea, to share the good news on primary night: he finished a strong second behind Paul Tsongas. A major hurdle had been passed as Clinton proved he could bounce back from voter doubts and attacks on his character. 18 February 1992

A worried Clinton and Stephanopoulos scan the morning papers on the plane from Seattle to Los Angeles. The "Comeback Kid" suddenly faced a new string of setbacks: Bob Kerrey won the South Dakota primary, in Maine Clinton had come in behind the voters' choice of "uncommitted," and Texas billionaire H. Ross Perot had invited the country to send him to Washington to "clean out the barn." 27 February 1992

Rattled that voters still confused him with Tsongas, Clinton vents his frustration to Stephanopoulos and Paul Begala, senior strategist, that the *Atlanta Constitution* had endorsed the former Massachusetts senator instead of him. Not afraid to disagree with his advisors or show his disappointment at times, Clinton described his management style during the race as that of "a very active, hands-on person," and his campaign style as "can-do, open, flexible." 2 March 1992

Following page: The Secret Service protects, and issues code names to, each of the qualified presidential candidates. Here, before flying to Baton Rouge to campaign for Super Tuesday, "Eagle" makes one last call from Columbia, South Carolina, while agent Rick Shields and staffers stand by. Bush was known as "Timber Wolf." 6 March 1992

Around midnight, after a rally in Hannibal, Missouri, Clinton calls Hillary at home as Bruce Lindsey stands by. "You give up a lot of your life, a lot of your privacy," Clinton has said of the process of running for president. "All this business about how everybody gets one free run at the White House, with nothing to lose—that's not true." 7 March 1992

Clinton takes questions from the press at the airport in Little Rock before flying to Dallas to debate Tsongas and Jerry Brown. Basing the campaign in the relative isolation of Little Rock—with no direct flights from major cities—gave the Clinton team distinct advantages: ready access to the governor's record, smaller demands from the press corps, and a spirited camaraderie among the young staff. 5 March 1992

The day before Super Tuesday, when eleven states would cast their votes in primaries, Clinton prepares for his upcoming media interviews from the Fort Lauderdale airport. With the candidates now down to three—Tsongas, Brown, and the governor from Arkansas—Clinton staffers refueled for the next leg of the primaries. 9 March 1992

Ever disciplined on the campaign trail, Carville takes a morning jog in Baton Rouge. Carville and his consulting partner, Paul Begala, had been sought after by two other Democratic candidates—Tom Harkin and Bob Kerrey—before teaming up with Clinton, who chose them in large part for Carville's fierce dedication and loyalty. "You pay for my head," he told Clinton, "and I throw my heart in for free."
7 March 1992

Clinton presses the flesh in tiny Stone Mountain on the day before the Georgia primary. By March, polls showed him winning as much as 80% of the black vote in the South. As one college student put it: "He understands the African-American community. He grew up in an environment where there was segregation, and he had an opportunity to see what it can do firsthand." 2 March 1992

Suddenly faced with last-minute changes in debate format, and minutes before going on air to face off with Tsongas and Brown in Dallas, Clinton and Hillary improvise a new strategy with Carville and Begala. Originally scheduled as a closely moderated event, ABC temporarily moved to a free-for-all format, switching back again just before the broadcast.
5 March 1992

Relaxing a bit after Super Tuesday, the Clintons bask in a rare moment alone in their hotel suite in Chicago following a late-night party for the staff. Opportunities to ease off while campaigning were rare, although Clinton had been known, after checking in to a hotel at midnight, to recruit three aides and play a few games of hearts to unwind. 13 March 1992

During a long campaign, the professional press corps faces the
same demons of fatigue and monotony as the candidates do.
Here *New York Times* photographer Jose Lopez and
Associated Press photographer Stephan Savoia try to lighten
the mood on the day before Super Tuesday. 9 March 1992

Before his upcoming debate with Jerry Brown, the advice for Clinton from his strategists is undeniably simple: Deputy Communications Director Bob Boorstin, Begala, and Stephanopoulos make it clear they want Clinton to stay with his own message, regardless of what the eccentric Brown might do or say. 28 April 1992

Perhaps nothing in politics matches the highs—or lows—of a presidential campaign, especially for campaign insiders whose decisions can make or break an election. Here Carville and Begala celebrate as Clinton scores points in a televised debate with Brown in New York, while Lindsey dances backstage to Clinton's introduction music as the candidate makes his entrance onstage. 5 April and 17 February 1992

After his big win on Super Tuesday, Clinton and Hillary are cheered in a Chicago hotel. The ups and downs of his race were beginning to stabilize; he had emerged as the Democratic frontrunner and proven his electability to the party's leaders. Clinton later described this turbulent time: "The last two weeks have been like a ride on the Coney Island Cyclone. Now that I've been through it, I've got to admit I've had a ball." 10 March 1992

Following page: In the ominous days after Clinton lost a critical Connecticut primary to Brown, the indefatigable candidate, ever flanked by the Secret Service, continues his nonstop stumping. Here he meets with local press after a late-night arrival back in Little Rock. 9 April 1992

After a rally in Buffalo, a Clinton die-hard shows where he stands. Showing his grit against raucous tabloid headlines and divisions in his own party, Clinton went on to win the New York primary, although Tsongas—officially out of the race since mid-March—finished a strong second. Rumors had been surfacing that, if he did well, Tsongas might reenter the race. He did not. 3 April 1992

Following page: Committed to building a new Democratic coalition, Clinton hosts Jesse Jackson in his Kansas City hotel suite, looking for solutions to the low turnout of southern Democrats in the early primaries. 25 April 1992

Clinton and Stanley Hill, a union leader in New York, play ball before a get-out-the-vote rally with Hill's union members. Spring brought the first challenge from Bush, who gave a major speech outlining his "reform agenda," and unearthed a new phenomenon: hordes of Perot supporters threatened to preempt Clinton's message of change. 4 April 1992

Attending a rally in Birmingham, but more concerned about
word of sudden rioting in Los Angeles after the Rodney King
verdict, Begala, Stephanopoulos, and Press Secretary Dee Dee
Myers gather news of the disaster. Three days later Clinton
flew to Los Angeles to meet with community leaders.
30 April 1992

In South Central Los Angeles, Clinton prays with church leaders in Pastor Chip Muarry's office before a meeting on healing the community's eruption of violence. "Underneath the anger," Clinton later said of America's growing disenfranchisement, "there's the sense that government works for the organized, the rich, and the powerful, not for ordinary folks." 3 May 1992

Clinton and Campaign Chairman Mickey Kantor find a quiet spot to talk on Capitol Hill before a day of discussions with members of Congress. "There's a generalized demand for shaking the system up," Clinton has said. "You're going to have a hundred new congressmen, and a lot of those who survive are going to have to promise to be more effective." 29 April 1992

Broadcasting via satellite from a hangar in Boston's Logan Airport, Clinton and Massachusetts Representative Joseph Kennedy thank supporters in Pennsylvania after that state's dicey primary. "People can't imagine what an effective presidency would be like anymore," Clinton has said. "What really ought to count is: What have you put yourself on the line for?" 28 April 1992

Following page: On this day, certainly, Wall Street was bullish on Clinton. With seven months until the election, polls showed Clinton running even with Bush, and having garnered nearly half of the 2,145 delegates he needed to win the Democratic nomination. 2 April 1992

Neighbors from Knickerbocker Avenue, a Hispanic
community in Brooklyn, wait to hear Clinton speak after he
had toured the area. Throughout the primaries, hoping to
inspire more faith in Democratic ideals, Clinton said, "To make
people believe in politics again you have to say: 'Here's how it's
going to be fair: It's going to work for everybody. But more
important, here's how it's going to work: We're going to restore
economic opportunity and a sense of progress.' " 4 April 1992

Clinton boards his campaign plane in Little Rock followed by Secret Service agent Billy Sauls. "You've got probably the deepest disillusionment with the American political system in my lifetime," Clinton said of the country's mood midspring. "It's much deeper than it was during Watergate." 12 May 1992

Following page: "Jim's my window on the world," Clinton says of his Little Rock barber, who was lowering Clinton's ears long before the candidate was elected the Arkansas governor in 1979—the youngest in the United States at age thirty-two. Secret Service agent Pete Dowling sits stoically through the haircut. 19 April 1992

The Clintons share a lunch at home on Memorial Day. "We love parenthood," Clinton has said, "and we're nuts about our kid in a wonderful way." 25 May 1992

Later that day, Bill and Hillary stroll the grounds of the Governor's Mansion together. "I believe the best way for me to demonstrate my character," Clinton has said, "is to make sure people know the whole story of my life, my work, my family, and what I'm fighting for in this election." 25 May 1992

55

Clinton rallies his home state in Benton on the night before the primaries in Arkansas, Idaho, and Kentucky. He won all three. While Democrats had lost five of the past six presidential elections, in part by aligning themselves too closely with special-interest groups and left-of-center issues, Clinton was emerging in this race as a more comfortable choice for moderate, middle-class Americans. 25 May 1992

James Carville looks on as Clinton tapes a new campaign ad from the grounds of the Governor's Mansion. During the later primaries, the candidate's top staff worked to reign in Clinton's far-ranging policy interests and to whittle down his message to three or four key themes. 26 May 1992

A few hours before playing for a live audience on *The Arsenio Hall Show*, Clinton practices "Heartbreak Hotel" on the balcony of his Santa Monica hotel. Later he joked with the show's band while rehearsing on the set, "If I screw up, play louder." Though he'd just won the California primary the day before—as well as primaries in four other states, guaranteeing enough delegates for the Democratic nomination—Clinton picked up a new surge of twentysomething voters with his stage banter and hip image that night. 3 June 1992

Following page: In the bright light of morning, Clinton's choice of running mate—made just the night before— not only still looked good; it dazzled. Tennessee Senator Al Gore catapulted the Democratic ticket into a new realm of appeal and credibility, and guaranteed that the campaign would focus on youth, energy, and smarts, themes that resounded from the moment the two first shook hands outside the Governor's Mansion after teaming up. 9 July 1992

About to burst on the scene as the first baby-boomer ticket in America, Clinton and Gore pause at the door of the Mansion before holding their first press conference as running mates. "I didn't seek this," Gore said of his candidacy. "I didn't expect it. I'm here for one simple reason: I love my country."
9 July 1992

That Clinton and Gore were simpatico from the start was to be expected: Ivy Leaguers from the South and fast-rising political moderates, both were "policy wonks" who thrived on debating intricate issues ad infinitum. Here Clinton walks Gore back to the Mansion guest house after a morning run. 10 July 1992

Already appearing as an unusually cohesive ticket just days after joining forces, Clinton and Gore stop in Carthage, Tennessee, Gore's hometown, to pitch their twin themes of hope and change. "I think fundamentally people in our generation are much more idealistic than a lot of others have been," Clinton said, "because we were raised to believe things were possible, that we can make a difference." 10 July 1992

During the Democrats' long, hot summer of stumping, Clinton and Gore took every opportunity to bring their families onstage. Though both Clinton's father and stepfather had passed away, Albert Gore, Sr., appeared in Carthage to share in his son's achievement. A three-term senator from Tennessee, the senior Gore once had his eye on the White House himself, and will always have his son's ear at home. 10 July 1992

Later that night in a crowd at Macy's, the Clinton family watches Governor Mario Cuomo give the convention's nominating speech. Clinton then walked across the street for an unexpected appearance, the first candidate since John F. Kennedy to come to the convention hall before the night of his formal speech. 15 July 1992

In New York, as Clinton rehearses his acceptance speech at a replica of the Democratic Convention's podium, Carville coaches him through the painstaking practice, making sure Clinton's message stays focused and his delivery sharp. "The idea that I'm a half-quart low has always worked to my advantage, has always kept the opposition just a little bit off guard," says the rough-hewn but exacting Carville, "so I've never done much to contradict it." 15 July 1992

Roy Spence, acceptance speech advisor, builds the candidate's energy and momentum in the downstairs holding room at Madison Square Garden as Clinton is introduced to the cheering crowd upstairs. 16 July 1992

Just hours before delivering his acceptance speech, Clinton tries to soothe his raw vocal cords, strained by endless rallies, in his hotel's steam room. Earlier that day, independent candidate Ross Perot had called a press conference, had proclaimed the Democratic Party "revitalized," and had dropped out of the race, leaving Clinton alone in the bid against Bush—or so he thought. "I feel humbled by the nomination," Clinton said. "It's an awesome responsibility." 16 July 1992

He survived a grueling primary race, attempts at character assassination, and an electorate more volatile than any in recent history to arrive at this point: center stage at the Democratic Convention to accept his party's nomination for president. And he came out swinging, blasting George Bush for squandering his "power to help America," vowing to focus on "our forgotten middle class," and introducing his New Covenant to put people first. 16 July 1992

71

"Clinton and Gore were like two guys at their twentieth reunion, who didn't really know each other in school, but just discovered they have a lot in common," Gore's staff director, Roy Neel, said after seeing them work together. Striking in their similarities and only nineteen months apart in age, the candidates look boyish as they emerge from Clinton's plane before appearing together at a picnic. Below, they attend the Sierra Club's endorsement rally, one of only two presidential endorsements the club has ever made. 7 and 4 September 1992

The 1992 campaign witnessed the revival of the whistle-stop tour, retooled to reach even deeper into grassroots America. Clinton and Gore, here about to be flagged down in Parrott, Georgia, set out on the first of six bus tours soon after the convention, hoping to win over rural voters considered small peanuts by other politicians. They appeared to succeed. "The more they see him," Media Consultant Mandy Grunwald said of her candidate, "the more they like him." 23 September 1992

Hustling from one stump to the next, Clinton knows he has little over a month to make his transition from winner of the Democratic Party's nomination to America's chief executive. But the man from Hope, Arkansas, here caught out in the rain in Georgia, had reason to be optimistic: he had won more primaries than any Democratic candidate since Lyndon Johnson in 1964. 23 September 1992

Keeping an unwavering eye on Clinton wherever he goes, Secret Service detail leader Tim Cahill steadies the flag in Indianola, Iowa. After the convention and first bus tour through the Ohio River valley, Clinton's polls surged to a two-to-one lead over Bush, a huge advantage that was short-lived but shocked the GOP nonetheless. 27 September 1992

The endless parade of speeches—sometimes four and five a day—appeared to energize, rather than wear down, the Democratic team. Clinton frequently invited Gore and Hillary to join him onstage, as he did in Cincinnati. 7 September 1992

Apparently ready for anything the campaign might send their way, Hillary and Al Gore's wife, Tipper, joke onstage in Albany, Georgia. "I feel like I have found somebody I have known forever," Tipper said of Hillary. "She is like a long-lost sister." 23 September 1992

Following page: Clinton listens to an intimate gathering of families in Eugene, Oregon, as they describe the hardships of losing their jobs in the logging industry. 16 September 1992

Fighting to control his emotions onstage, Clinton is welcomed by long, thunderous applause on his return to New Hampshire. The Manchester auditorium was filled with people who had been instrumental in his early campaign, those first supporters who had encouraged him to continue running despite all the trials he'd endured. 26 September 1992

As he continued to ask for America's trust, Clinton began to focus his message on the issue of greatest concern to voters: the economy. "People are dying to believe again, they desperately want this country to work again," Clinton said that summer as he pushed through the South, recently staunch GOP territory; here he rallies the crowd in Columbia, South Carolina. 5 September 1992

Nicknamed "Elvis" by the press after he had imitated the Mississippi singer, Clinton continued to draw massive young crowds, like this one in Madison, Wisconsin, as the campaign moved into the fall. Even one-on-one with Gore, here on the bus to Orlando, the candidate works the crowd.
1 and 5 October 1992

Following page: Stalled at a crossroads in his campaign—still unable to lure Bush into the debate arena and plateauing just ahead in the polls—Clinton faced a daunting task: to win over voters, in an age of anti-politics, without appearing too political. 23 September 1992

As Perot sinks millions into his crude pointer-and-chart
infomercials, Clinton risks appearing among the high-rises of
Houston. Home state of both of his rivals, Texas was not
expected to be won over by Clinton. Here Governor Ann
Richards and Senator Lloyd Bentsen join him onstage.
31 October 1992

Security was integral to a campaign that touched down in as many as three states a day, and one based on Stephanopoulos' strategy to get Clinton out in public continually, "in as many unfiltered forums as possible—to get people watching the real thing, rather than something that's reported on." Here Secret Service agents stand guard in a crowd in Pueblo, Colorado, one carrying a disguised bullet-proof shield. 21 October 1992

The debate schedule finally set, advisor Michael Sheehan coaches Clinton as they review a tape of the candidate in preparation for an unprecedented three-way presidential debate; independent Ross Perot had suddenly reentered the race. Later, wearing a "bomber" jacket Hillary had given him for their anniversary, Clinton is directed by Sheehan to face the camera while talking to "Bush" in a practice session.
10 and 11 October 1992

Aware of the power of image—and reminded that a young JFK had won his debate with Nixon by giving the public their first good look at him as a stately candidate—Clinton put himself through rigorous critique before the first debate. Monitoring his logic, his phrasing, his tone of voice, even his gestures, Clinton's team works to expose the best side of their candidate.
8 October 1992

Suddenly left with little to do, Stephanopoulos, and Media
Consultants Frank Greer and Harry Thomason sit tight while
Clinton is being made up for the first debate; Mickey Kantor
relaxes by tossing a ball across the room. 11 October 1992

"Better'n grits" was how James Carville would later describe the first debate, though at the time, he grimaced at each attack on his candidate and fought to frame each answer right along with Clinton. More than seventy million Americans watched the first debate, hosted by Washington University in St. Louis.
11 October 1992

During the debate, after Bush assaulted Clinton's patriotism—
and Clinton shot back his answer—Stephanopoulos reacts to
an apparent bull's-eye. Later, Clinton signs autographs beside
Ron Brown, Democratic National Chairman. The media
generally agreed that Perot won the debate with his down-
home talk, that Bush lost a critical opportunity, and that
Clinton gave a solid, exquisitely prepared performance.
11 October 1992

Following page: The first debate behind him and still
ahead in the polls, Clinton takes an early morning run
through Colonial Williamsburg, Virginia. 15 October 1992

Clinton's style of political discourse emerged during the campaign as
essentially conversational: he could listen to and engage with his
audience as well as speechify. And in the second debate—an untried
talk-show format with 209 undecided voters—his ability to respond
empathetically to questions from the audience would prove critical.
Here Clinton consults with Gore and Gene Sperling,economic advisor.
26 and 14 October 1992

Still working to hear the subtle currents underneath the electorate's ebb and flow, Stephanopoulos gathers in his last research on the day before the second debate. The first campaign staffer hired by Clinton, Stephanopoulos displayed an uncanny ability to predict Clinton's own thinking on political strategy and to shape a campaign that would suit the candidate. 14 October 1992

Buoyed by the cheers of his debate staff, Clinton moves
quickly down the hall from his holding room, about to go
onstage for the second presidential debate in Richmond.
The results: many thought Clinton was the winner; he was
clearly the most at ease in the informal, give-and-take style
he'd perfected in the primaries. 15 October 1992

Clinton and Bush, already polarized by their political
ideologies and by their different approaches to earning
trust from the American people, stand remote as they await
the start of the third debate. Separated by a full partition,
neither man, at this moment, can see or hear
the other. 19 October 1992

Bush gathered steam in the third debate, finally showing
his focus and conviction, while Perot's pat metaphors
began to sound as hollow as a cleaned-out barn. Clinton
handily fielded lead interviewer Jim Lehrer's questions
before a record audience of ninety-one million viewers.
19 October 1992

In an election crowded with talk shows, voter call-in shows, and the promise of electronic town meetings, the average American moved center stage to set all three candidates' agendas. Clinton started the town-meeting idea in New Hampshire, in response to the cynicism he saw: "I think the American people are saying: 'Pox on both your houses. This deal's not working for the average person. We may not know exactly what changes we want, but we want some fundamental changes.' " It's clearly a "people" campaign here in Madison, Wisconsin, and Wilmington, Delaware. 1 and 12 October 1992

"We're not electing a king here, we're electing a president," Clinton told supporters, though crowds at the farmer's market in St. Louis and in Louisville, Kentucky, treated him like royalty, jostling and straining to get close for just a moment. "I feel confident about the election," he said. "I think we're on the right side of history. . . . But I don't feel ordained, and I don't think the results of this election are foreordained. It's going to be a very, very difficult election." 3 and 18 October 1992

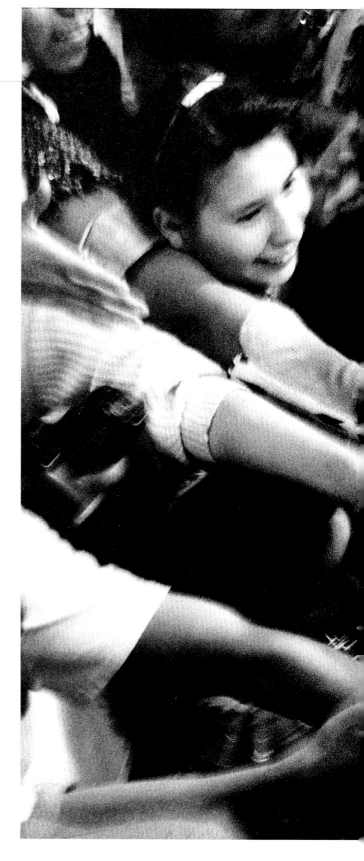

Nine-year-old Vicki White, who had asked to meet Clinton before undergoing surgery for bone disease, gets some gentle encouragement in a tête-à-tête not open to the press. "It's a sort of legacy that my grandparents left to me," Clinton had said, "the idea that if you get beat down, you just get up again, and that you find something to be grateful for every day."
9 October 1992

Rarely interviewed or photographed by the press, Chelsea Clinton is, says her father, "much more tough-minded and savvy than I ever dreamed." She's been raised by two parents who have fully embraced the notion of autonomy for young people: several years ago, Chelsea was asked by her parents which spiritual faith she felt moved to follow; she chose to explore her mother's Methodist over her father's Baptist religion. 17 October 1992

The candidate gets a farewell card from one of his Secret Service details on the last flight of their three-week watch over his campaign. Another team would step in to cover Clinton until the election. 22 October 1992

"My marriage is not a creation of any external force," Hillary has said. "It is between Bill Clinton and me. And it will be between us whether he wins or loses, whatever happens." The Clintons rally for serve after a speech in Milwaukee. 20 October 1992

"There's an enormous amount of hope out there," Clinton has said. "This has always been an incurably optimistic country." The youngest man to win a major party endorsement since John F. Kennedy, Bill Clinton at forty-six appeared about to succeed at what no Democrat had managed for years: inspiring a "re-United States."
31 October 1992

A man who goes to great lengths to touch people in a personal way, Clinton had ultimately created a new kind of campaign, one that succeeded, in his words, by "going back to the people, trying to be accessible, and giving the people their government back." Clinton introduces himself to a kitchen worker in Chamblee, Georgia, and reaches through football stadium steps to shake hands with a beckoning fan in Decatur, Georgia.
31 October 1992

Following pages: Embarking on his last full day of campaigning, a nine-state day that would have taken most people a week to get through, Clinton reacts to lyrics sung onstage by Jerry Jeff Walker in Fort Worth and greets voters by flashlight in McAllen, Texas.
3 November 1992

Finally heading home to Little Rock, Clinton still has
work to do, polishing two speeches: the one he'll deliver
stoically if he should lose, and the one that will carry his
first words to the nation should he win. A carefully modest
frontrunner during the last weeks of the race, Clinton
allows himself one small indulgence for a campaign well
run. 3 November 1992

Along with his family, Clinton emerges from his
campaign plane and faces a crowd of staffers and media,
not yet knowing whether this is the beginning or the end,
or whether he'll ever again be this close to an American
presidency. 3 November 1992

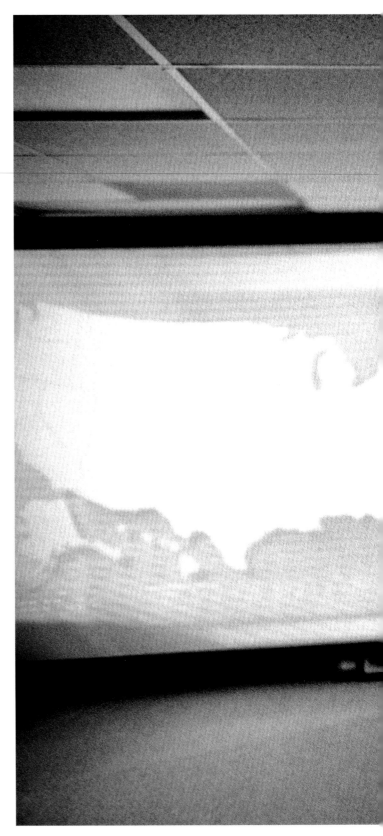

From the downstairs office of the Governor's Mansion,
Clinton watches as the election results come in; here he
learns that he's won New Jersey, Colorado, and Maine.
In the end, he garnered 370 electoral votes to Bush's 168;
Perot took none. 3 November 1992

As he watches the last polls close, Clinton has made history as he becomes America's forty-second president, the first from a little state called Arkansas, a man who, after this day, will always believe in a place called Hope.
3 November 1992

Before a crowd that had been anticipating Clinton's appearance for hours, two staffers pull open the doors of the Old State House in Little Rock and then melt away, leaving clear the path for the Clintons' walk onstage as the nation's new First Family. "With high hopes and brave hearts and massive numbers," Clinton said that night in his victory speech, "the American people have voted to make a new beginning." 3 November 1992

"I remind you again tonight, my fellow Americans, that this victory was more than a victory of party; it was a victory for the people who work hard and play by the rules, a victory for the people who feel left out and left behind and want to do better. . . . I accept tonight the responsibility that you have given me to be the leader of this, the greatest country in human history. I accept it with a full heart and a joyous spirit." 3 November 1992

Epilogue

Michael Kramer

In the beginning he was an unknown candidate running against an unbeatable president, and for a while it went downhill from there. How many times did he die? It is hard to recall. "Several at least," Bill Clinton himself said shortly before he rose for good. "Maybe more than several. But I always came back, didn't I?"

Politicians radiate impressions. Few outsiders know their inner cores. In different times and places, personalities connect for different reasons. Clinton prevailed, it seems to me, because of his toughness. Not tough in the sense of ruthless or boorish, but rather tough in the sense of purpose, of mission and meaning business. Tough like a machine that has been stripped of frills, ready for action—action in mind and in thought.

To those lucky enough to have caught his act in person during the campaign, Clinton projected energy and speed. Believing he could do the job better than anyone else, he moved briskly: What's the question? Here's the response. His thoughts were clear, going immediately to the heart of the problem, a tough yet supple mind at the height of its power.

To label Clinton a survivor is to state the obvious, so often did victory seem improbable. But recall the course of his travails: Gennifer Flowers, the draft, the charges that he waffled on the issues and massaged his rhetoric to conform to the expectations of his varied audiences. Others have been hobbled by less. Clinton tucked it in, bit his lip (an expression that signals deep thought, extreme satisfaction, or consuming anger; an observer rarely knows which), and plowed on.

In retrospect, his fellow Democrats were as savage as the Republicans: Paul Tsongas called him a "pander bear," Bob Kerrey predicted the opposition would "open him up like a soft-shelled peanut," and Jerry Brown struck at his wife. A consensus formed early and resurfaced regularly throughout the long winter and spring of primaries: Clinton was hopelessly crippled. It was only a matter of time. The man was dead but didn't know it. Soon, it was said with confidence, a true heavyweight would emerge to rescue the party from another inglorious defeat, from the Republican incumbent who had sworn to do whatever it took to be reelected. But the would-be saviors stayed home, the rivals faded, and the unbeatable president ran a hapless, unfocused campaign. In the end only the dead man lived, his long march a triumph of preparation, tenacity, and drive. Luck, too, played a role—it always does—but as the baseball mogul Branch Rickey once observed, luck is often "the residue of design."

All campaigns have their moments and many are remembered for decades. But "Bill and Al's Excellent Adventure" was special, proof of H. L. Mencken's assertion that covering an American presidential campaign is "better than watching the best circus that ever was."

Things that are well made are long in the crafting. As a young boy, Bill Clinton played touch football in his yard and sometimes pretended he was a Kennedy on the White House lawn. A few years later he was on that lawn, shaking hands with the Kennedy who lived there, vowing privately, we now know, that it would be his house one day. Two devastating political defeats and several more victories helped him hone his political skills, and by 1988 he seemed ready. He passed that year, but in the years to follow he burnished his centrist credentials with the single-mindedness that has characterized his life. Ronald Reagan was gone but his legacy endured. The nation's political ideology had tilted rightward and Clinton went with the flow. He would offer an activist politics but it was always rooted in the center. In tone and content he sometimes appeared as an endangered species—as a moderate Republican. He tacked to the left to meet the primary challenges of Paul Tsongas and Jerry Brown, and he sounded populist chords against Bush when his innate strategic sense told him it was wise. But in every major pronouncement he stayed square in the middle— where the votes were.

We will learn soon enough what was act and what is real. Whether or not he challenges us—as he promises—we will most assuredly challenge him. But we know something else already. We know something of the man. As the campaign proved Clinton's toughness, it also revealed his tenderness. Two moments tell the tale.

Everyone in politics heard the rumors: Clinton, it was said with force but without proof, had a "wandering eye." To run when the memory of Gary Hart was fresh seemed foolish, even reckless. But the Clintons are not fools. Armed with his wife's support and his own resolve, Clinton launched a preemptive strike in September 1991 at a breakfast with journalists in Washington: he admitted his marriage had been rocky, but insisted that it was now rock solid. Hillary Clinton's mere presence spoke volumes: if I'm sticking by him, she didn't need to say, it is no one else's business.

For five months, the campaign proceeded without incident. Actually, it soared; Mario Cuomo refused to play and Clinton became the annointed frontrunner even before a single vote had been cast. But then in February, on the eve of the New Hampshire primary, it all came unglued. A former television newscaster and cabaret singer named Gennifer Flowers alleged a twelve-year affair with Clinton. The days that followed were hell. Flowers had tapes! They were doctored, it turned out, but Mark Twain's adage never seemed more apt: a lie is around the world before the truth gets out of bed. A statement was needed, Clinton aides said; or some surrogates could strike back. But Clinton knew that only he could defend himself and still survive. He chose *60 Minutes* as his forum. A makeshift studio was constructed at a Boston hotel a few floors above a room where the Association of Matrimonial Lawyers was meeting. Under relentless questioning, the Clintons performed well, but the highlight of their appearance never made the air. Midway through the shoot, a bank of lights held high on a pipe came crashing to the ground about a foot from Hillary. Clinton instantly grabbed his wife and pulled her to him. They embraced as Clinton gently stroked her hair. "It's okay," he said. "It's okay; it's over. Don't worry." That single incident, which the public never saw, said more about their marriage than even they could ever say.

A few weeks later, at a senior citizens' center, Clinton gave another policy-laden speech. The audience wanted specifics and Clinton delivered. "Read my plan," he intoned repeatedly, but those who heard him didn't have to. Clinton knew the details, and those with the stamina to hear him out heard them all. As the event ended—behind schedule as always—a frail woman leaning on an oversized wooden cane came forward to speak about health care. The candidate's aides signaled "enough," but Clinton lingered. The crowd dispersed. The traveling press corps drifted away, and the Secret Service agents relaxed. Clinton and the woman talked for about twenty minutes. He spoke but he also listened. He had yet to flesh out his health care proposals fully, and he seized the opportunity to learn as well as preach. "How does the visiting nurse system work here?" he asked. "How quickly are the payments made? Do they overcharge? Does Medicare pay for your cane? What about your medication? They overcharge for that, don't they?" When the woman couldn't answer, Clinton seemed incredulous. "You should know these things," he said quietly. "You realize it's everyone else's tax dollars that are involved," he added—toughly but tenderly. "I mean, we're happy to pay," he said. "We owe you that. But you should make sure we're not being ripped off. You agree, don't you?" "Well, I suppose," she said a bit sheepishly, looking down. Clinton touched her arm gingerly and smiled. "I tell you what," she said; "I'll find out." "Good," he said, "and write me when you do." Afterward, the woman seemed perplexed. "He was more interested than my son," she said. "He's not Jewish, is he?" "No, why?" a journalist asked. "Well, he seems like such a *mensch*. Can a *mensch* be president?"

Campaigns reach a point where those who run, those who assist, and those who follow come to share a strange unreality. Exhaustion becomes their common bond. The polls direct their travels as the candidates search for the "Magic 270," the electoral votes needed for victory. At the end of Clinton's last marathon, a grueling nine-state, twenty-nine-hour journey to one airport rally after another, only the pilot really knew where they were. Clinton's voice was gone; he managed a few words but Hillary did most of the talking. In Cincinnati, on the morning before election day, Clinton ate a chili dog as he greeted the crowd, shaking hands and signing autographs so quickly that he ignored the sauce splattered on his face. An aide handed him a napkin. He autographed it.

At the Tryed Stone Baptist Church, Clinton requested a "spiritual prayer," which the Reverend Anderson Culbreath delivered as the choir sang "I Don't Believe He Brought Me This Far to Leave Me." At 2:10 A.M. on election day, on his way to Albuquerque from Fort Worth, the nation's first true policy-wonk president talked to his aides about converting cars to natural gas. The plane landed at 3:00 A.M. The New Mexico crowd had been waiting for hours and would have to wait twenty-eight minutes longer. Clinton had disappeared into the bathroom to change his shirt and had fallen asleep. Finally, after a sun-up rally in Colorado, there was nothing left to do. "It's been a long ride," Clinton said. "I'm just glad it's over." But it wasn't, quite. Before he won, Clinton said that he knew what he would do first when the campaign ended: "I am going to thank God." And when he arrived home in Little Rock as the first exit polls confirmed that it had all been worth it, that is exactly what Bill Clinton did.

"You can trust us to wake up every day remembering the people we saw on the bus trips, the people we saw in the town meetings, the people we touched at the rallies, the people who had never voted before, the people who hadn't voted in twenty years, the people who'd never voted for a Democrat, the people who had given up hope, all of them together saying we want our future back. And I intend to help give it to you. . . .

If we have no sense of community, the American dream will continue to wither. Our destiny is bound up with the destiny of every American. We're all in this together, and we will rise or fall together. That has been my message to the American people for the past thirteen months and it will be my message for the next four years.

Together we can do it. Together we can make the country that we love everything it was meant to be. I still believe in a place called Hope."

President-elect BILL CLINTON
Little Rock, Arkansas
3 November 1992

ACKNOWLEDGMENTS

This project could not have been accomplished without the help of many people.

First and foremost I would like to thank Clinton's press secretary, Dee Dee Myers, for all her help in securing this endeavor. She was instrumental in convincing the staff it would work and in keeping the project going all year.

To Picture Editor Michele Stephenson and Associate Picture Editor Rick Boeth, both from TIME, thanks for your unwavering support, both financial and otherwise, all year. And Rick, sorry you had the task of having to look at every frame I shot for the magazine.

On the road, thanks to the following people from the Clinton campaign: Bruce Lindsey, George Stephanopoulos, Paul Begala, Rodney Slater, James Carville, Wendy Smith, Degee Wilhelm, Adam Sohn, Lorraine Voles, Steve Rabinowitz, Bob McNeely, and, of course, my sushi partner in crime, Steve "Scoop" Cohen. You all were great traveling companions—we did have some fun out there. Thanks to all the folks at Clinton headquarters for scheduling information, including Ethan Zingler, Mora Segal, Stephanie Street, Julia Payne, and the cast of thousands. At the Governor's Mansion, special thanks to Mark Allen for your laughter and good cheers; the catfish dinners weren't bad either.

To the staff at the Capital Hotel in Little Rock, thanks for always having my usual room ready and making me feel at home away from home when we overnighted in Arkansas. Thanks, Patrice.

Last but not least, special thanks to my girlfriend, Beth, who had to endure my being gone most of the year. Thinking of her and our life in Stinson Beach helped keep me going during the long hours of the campaign. Her spiritual support was essential to this project. Thanks, Beth. I love you very much.

Oh, yeah: Thanks, Elvis, I know you're alive.

P. F.

Epicenter Communications would like to thank
the following friends and advisors for their contributions to this project:

Alan Abrams	Acey Harper	Michael Morris
Marc Bailin	Holly Herman	Henry Muller
Jackie Barndollar	Ellen Herrick	William T. Naythons
Milton Batalion	Caroline Herter	Nanscy Neiman
Sandy Berger	Arnie Kanter	Peter Pappass
Diane Burns	Mickey Kantor	Howard Paster
Stanley Burns	Suzanne Keating	Daniel Paul
Ingrid Castro	Laurence J. Kirshbaum	Eugene Pierce
Philip Castro	Rebecca Kondos	Tom Rielly
Ray Cave	Harvey-Jane Kowal	Nancy Rosenthal
Michael Cerre	Ron Kriss	Steve Ross
David Cohen	Avis LaVelle	William Sarnoff
Sashka T. Dawg	Carla Levdar	Deborah Schneider
Sandro Diani	Gerald M. Levin	Eli Segal
Maureen Mahon Egen	Bev Lindsey	David Seldin
Jeff Eller	Charles Marcus	Vincent Severino
Karen Ewing	Stewart McBride	Rick Smolan
Eleanor Freedman	Marsha McCoskrie	Rebecca Swanston
Jamie Gangell	Jeanne McCulloch	Judith Thurman
John Gage	Kevin McVea	Gordon W. Tucker
Mary Ellen Glynn	Keith Metzger	Thomas Whatley
Anne Hamilton	Phillip Moffitt	Miriam Winocour

The Clinton Advance and RON Teams

The flight attendants and crews of "Air Elvis"

The traveling press corps

The staff at Worldwide Travel

SuperMac Technology, Inc.

The TIME-LIFE black-and-white lab,
with special thanks to John Downey

About this book:

All photographs were made with Ilford XP-2, Fuji 1600 Neopan, and Kodak P3200 film
using Leica and Canon cameras.

This book was created using QuarkXpress on Apple Macintosh IIci computers
equipped with SuperMac 21-inch color monitors and SuperMac Thunder accelerated graphic cards.
All images were scanned on a Hewlett Packard ScanJet IIc using Ofoto scanning software from Lightsource.
Final layouts for proofing were printed on Apple Laserwriter IINTXs equipped with Adobe Postscript software.
The book was stored on MicroNet magneto-optical drive cartridges,
and the final layout delivered for printing on Syquest 44 MB cartridges.

Photographic printing by Bill Pierce
Duotone separations by JAC Lithographers, West Babylon, New York
Printing by R. R. Donnelley & Sons, Willard, Ohio